THE BIG CHILL

OF JUNE 2006

PENGUIN BOOKS

Compiled by Jeff Grigor from photographs by the people of Canterbury

THE BIG CHILL OF JUNE 2006

It's been credited with bringing communities together, but no one in Canterbury knew when they awoke to a white morning on 12 June 2006 that it would be another two weeks before life would return to normal.

It was the worst snowfall Mid- and South Canterbury had seen since 1946 and like that one, the snow event of 2006 will become legend and will be talked about around the dinner table for years to come. The extent of the snowfall was far-reaching. People were completely cut off. There was no going to neighbouring areas for help as the snowstorm had been unusually widespread.

As snowfall went, however, it was not that deep. In Timaru, reports put snowfall at 25 centimetres, in Geraldine it was up to 40 centimetres and in the Aoraki/Mt Cook National Park it was 200 centimetres, prompting an avalanche warning. But it was wet snow – heavy and the type that clumped together.

In the coastal regions of south and mid-Canterbury the snow fell on a district in which the infrastructure was not geared up to withstand it. Power poles buckled and broke, lines stretching and snapping under the snow's weight; roofs caved in; telecommunications were lost or at best disrupted; roads and schools were closed; and businesses couldn't do business. In Geraldine, customers were warned to stay out of the central business district as the weight of snow threatened to bring down shopfront verandahs. The snow even changed the golden sands of Caroline Bay in Timaru to bright white – an occurrence few could recall happening before.

Water supplies and sewerage plants rely on electricity. Modern clean, green septic tanks need it to pump waste. Rural homes and stock systems need it to bring water in, and even for those in town, boiling the water was necessary as the chlorination treatment plants had ceased to work.

As tree branches succumbed to the dead weight of snow, they could be heard cracking like bullet shots, and in some cases whole trees tumbled over. Refuse stations around the district soon filled with mountains of greenery for their composting programmes, and parks, reserves and sportsgrounds remained closed for weeks as the danger from falling branches put them out of bounds. Fallen trees blocked walking tracks. Even the birds found it hard to survive and many didn't, as frozen snow covered their food sources.

Farmers were forced to bring stock down from higher pastures, cutting tracks to reach them. Because there was no phone access they were not able to check on neighbours or work out the best way to deal with an emergency. They had to carry out any urgent work straightaway and ensure stock was cared for before going anywhere else.

Dairy farmers were left with no way of milking their cows. Fortunately it was not high season, but for those on the town milk supply their cows were still producing. Each of those farmers will lose thousands of dollars this season through reduced production. The effects are predicted to roll over to next season. The cost to the country and the central South Island will be immense. Far greater, say the farmers, than the cost to Auckland of its loss of power for five hours on the same day. The figure tossed about for Auckland was $70 million.

Farmers in the Clandeboye region at least had a hero. Local electrician Gary Moir got hold of a generator which he transported around the five farms in the district. Milking was 16 hours apart instead of 12 and sometimes the farmers were up milking at 1 a.m. or 2 a.m. – when the generator arrived. But they all take their hats off to Mr Moir who worked continuously, grabbing a couple of hours sleep in the truck until it was time to move on to the next farm.

Add to this the plight of beef and sheep farmers. Sheep were particularly vulnerable to the snow. They needed high-quality feed like baleage, or hay and green feed. Unfortunately winter green feed had been decimated in the snow. Farm feed stocks dwindled fast as the snow had come harder, earlier and to lower levels. There was no thaw for many parts of the district a month later. To help supplement the feed situation, farmers used tractors with blades to cut trenches through the snow so sheep could reach the grass below to graze. But in July, with the rams due out and in some areas lambing not that far off, the situation looked much more dire.

And spare a thought for the pigs. One farmer said he could not get to feed his 800 pigs because conditions were so atrocious on the first day. Usually they were fed by an automatic computerised feeder, which of course needed power.

For rural people, even those on the outskirts of the urban areas, it was chaos. Many lifestyle farmers don't have the machinery found on other farms – their small tractors were no use against the snow drifts. Their septic tanks weren't working either.

About a third, or 10,000, of South Canterbury's power users lost their power. Another 10,000 Mid-Canterbury homes were without power too. Some were without it for hours, many for days, many for two weeks and a handful for a little longer. But they are a resourceful lot in Canterbury and as long as they had another source of heat, most got by. It's amazing how easy it is to cook a curry on the firebox of a log burner.

There was a rush on generators as homeowners tried to buy or hire them, and gas burners were purchased to cook the family meal. Candles and batteries were in short supply and for a while could not be bought for love nor money. New stocks were desperately ordered and eagerly awaited by those in outlying townships and larger urban areas as well. For many, the transistor radio was the only contact with the outside world. People listened to it to hear when power would be restored and how others in the community were coping.

The phones were more or less restored within four days, but as the days went by and the power system remained down, people started to understand there was no quick fix to the chaos and they needed to look for better solutions. Rural people were forced to boil water on their wood fires or gas barbecues and fill the bath to hand wash clothes. One woman, without power for 10 days, said she felt like she had wet hands the whole time.

There were also medical emergencies. People on some home treatments needed electricity to work their machines; they had to find their way to towns and public hospitals to ensure their treatment continued.

Some elderly people were shifted into rest homes because they only had electric heating. Some families moved in with other family members and some into motels. Motels in Temuka offered free accommodation to people without power and during the eleventh day the Timaru District Council offered to pay for motels for its ratepayers still without power. About 33 families, over 100 people, took up the offer. Businesses chipped in to help make it an occasion. Meals, chocolates and passes to the movies were provided.

Transport companies cleared snow and driveways for no charge. In one instance, the head cook at an old person's home in Timaru got her husband to take her to work on his tractor.

But right from the start it was the four-wheel drive club that deserved accolades for their assistance to the South Canterbury district. From the first day they ferried hospital staff to and from work; carted round Timaru police officers who did not have their own four-wheel drive vehicles, as they checked on people isolated in the snow; and offered their services in any way they could.

Temuka Salvation Army officer Alison Anderson had nothing but praise for the club members: 'The Salvation Army made hot meals to deliver around the district. One afternoon we were asked for 130 meals – 100 went to Temuka and 30 to Geraldine. It was no bother at all, even at such short notice. The women were great. The four-wheel drive club drove us around so we could get the meals where they were supposed to go, and helped us to deliver baking and goodwill bags, with little things in them to let people know they weren't alone. They weren't forgotten; people were thinking of them. We couldn't have done it without the four-wheel drive club.'

Mrs Anderson said it was very rewarding being able to help people and said she had been amazed at the generosity of the public. There had been grave fears for the elderly and those with young families during the storm and its aftermath. Being able to go door-knocking had allayed some of those fears.

One of the district's civil defence coordinators Graeme Broker said he had been overwhelmed by the big-heartedness of people and they way they looked out for their neighbours.

At the same time, having that can-do ethic may have worked against getting help faster. He said people were so busy looking after each other that no one had sent out messages asking for help, and that is why it took so long to find out the extent of the problems some people were facing.

If there has been any criticism it has been about the length of time it has taken for roads and footpaths to be cleared, and the failure of the telecommunications system. It's hoped the debriefings will shed some light on how to do things better in the future.

Some farmers believe lessons need to be learned and farms need to become more self-sufficient. There has been criticism that successive socialist governments are breeding a nation of sissies that can't make decisions for themselves but rely on governments and authorities to get them out of a bind.

Others believe that emergency planning needs to be from the bottom up rather than the top down as it is now. In other words, when there is an emergency someone in a street or a district has to be responsible for checking on whether people are okay, and then work with others to see how the available equipment in the area can be used to the greatest advantage.

But it was not all gloom. Not only had community spirit returned but the district was picture postcard perfect. Snow swathed branches – those still intact that is – hung prettily off spouting and with the full moon the nights were so bright that it somehow compensated for the lack of electric light. It was truly beautiful.

People skied to work. Snowman competitions were held with most street corners having at least one snowman holding court.

Dogs slid over on the ice looking dumbfounded and of course it was all crash landings for ducks on ponds.

Children took part in snow fights and went tobogganing. A few young hoons probably risked their lives being towed along behind cars. But police reported a quiet time. A few people trying to take their cars where they shouldn't caused some frustrations. On the whole, police say there was little crime despite alarms not working because of no power; probably because, like everybody else, the crims had a hard time getting around. Perhaps, though, it was because like everyone else they were touched with a bit of that community spirit that has so overawed people in the area.

And we can't forget some of the rural posties, acting as lifelines for their isolated populations, who say they will never forget their actions. The posties were their only link with the outside world. Some of these posties battled through very difficult conditions just to help keep people in touch and make sure nothing was amiss.

So if we can say nothing else about the snow of June 2006, we can say it was the event that invigorated neighbourhoods, helped people rediscover the art of conversation, saw families comfortably chatting around the fire by candlelight at night, brought back community and showed how little we have without it.

Helen Pickering
July 2006

Top: The corner of
Stafford and Strathallan
Streets, Timaru.
Wendy & Phil Smith
Right: Talbot Street,
Geraldine.
Daryll Mahan

Top: King Street, Temuka, looking north.
C & V Howey
Left: Heavy snow in the carpark in front of the town clock, Ashburton.
Kelly Haines

Top: Levels, looking towards Timaru, 15 June 2006.
Jeff Mill
Right: From St Mary's church clocktower, looking west over Pleasant Point.
Jeff Tollan

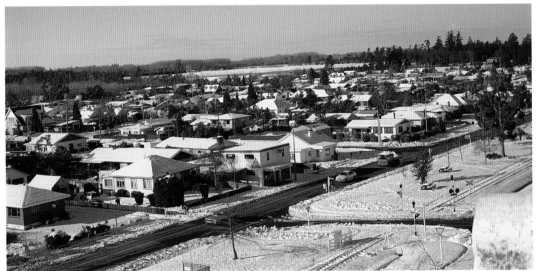

Top: A Hagglund BV206 all-terrain vehicle owned by the International Antarctic Centre, Christchurch, contracted to inspect the power lines by a power-line transmission company. The picture on the **left** is of Porters Pass, part of the area being inspected, where the snow was up to one metre deep. The Hagglund was the only vehicle capable of travelling on that stretch of road for over 24 hours.
Roger Harris

Top left: Police roadblock at Winchester. The traffic was turned back as the road to Christchurch was closed.
Kate & Roger Patterson
Top right: Carl McIntyre beside fallen power lines, Rugby Street, Timaru.
Paul Webb
Right: An Electricity Ashburton truck stuck in the roundabout, Netherby shopping centre, Ashburton.
Priska Ross

Top: Snow being cleared, Flatman Crescent, Geraldine. *Sharon Attwood*
Far left and left: Sicon removing snow from roadside in Temuka, 20 June 2006. *Jeanette Smith*

Top: In these conditions even four-wheel drive vehicles have to take care. This one is being towed back onto the road near Fairlie.
Yvonne Marshall

Far right: No flying today. The 7.00 a.m. flight to Wellington still waiting to depart from Richard Pearse airport, mid-afternoon 12 June.
Matthew Dey

Right: Temuka Fire Brigade on duty.
Debbie & Brian Doake

Right-hand page:
Hoar frost at Sailors Cutting, Lake Benmore.
Rosslyn Hood

Top: Mackenzie Country looking picture-postcard perfect.
Rosslyn Hood
Bottom left: A once cone-shaped conifer irreparably damaged by the snow, Winchester.
Annette Bray
Bottom right: Autumnalis flowering through the snow, Otipua Road, Timaru.
Ann Hawes

Left: Catastrophic damage to an oak tree in the Melcombe Street park, Ashburton. *Christine Wilson*
Top right: Linesmen on the job at Waitohi. *Megan Inwood*
Bottom right: Snow-damaged transformer on Pendarves Farm, Rules Road, Pendarves, Ashburton. *Thomas Duncan*

Left: It sure is cold.
Franka Morik
Top right: Kune kune
in Sterndale Valley,
Pleasant Point district.
Nigel Gamble
Bottom right: Gemma
the labrador delivering
the *Timaru Herald*,
Timaru.
Susie & Gerald Morton
Left-hand page: You
would have to be mad.
The ultimate polar bear
swim, Lake Tekapo.
Franka Morik

Top: Dog Rock,
Rock Farm, Cave,
South Canterbury.
P & A Ulrich
Right: Kinneswood,
a holiday home in
Blandswood.
Alan Macnaughtan

Corrugated snow, a
result of snow sliding
off the roof days after
the big fall, Temuka.
Top: *Charlie Jelley*
Left: *Barry Hiscock*
Far left: Icy
waterfall, Barker holiday
residence, Fairlie.
Warren Barker

Top: Al McCabe
snow-raking on Godley
Peaks Station, above
Lake Tekapo.
Haidee & Al McCabe
Right: Al McCabe
saving a snowbound
merino.
Haidee & Al McCabe

Top left: Tragic consequences of the storm, Pendarves Farm, Pendarves, Ashburton. *Thomas Duncan*

Top right: Just another problem the farmers faced – how to open your gate in snow deeper than half a metre. *Haidee & Al McCabe*

Bottom left: The storm proved to be too much even for this stag. *Peter Wilkinson*

Bottom right: Feeding out to the Perendales using the Sno-Cat, on Peter Cooke's property, Rockdale, Totara Valley. *Nigel Gamble*

Top: No rest for the silage wagon on the Lemon's farm, Lauriston, Mid-Canterbury.
Kerri Lemon
Right: The old and the new – Clydesdales versus the silage wagon. Geoffrey Cottle driving, with Sophie Cross from Nova Scotia Canada, Lyalldale, South Canterbury.
Kirsty Keen
Right-hand page: Winter wonderland. Early morning, Ashburton.
Margaret Clifford

Top left: Peter Cooke of Rockdale, Totara Valley was continuously in action with his Sno Cat, helping linesmen to reach power outages and helping neighbours to cut tracks for access to stock in difficult terrain. He gave selflessly of his time and machinery. Timaru Herald *sent in by Mrs W Weir*

Top right: Scott Haines clearing his driveway, helped by Meg, Coniston Water, Ashburton. *Kelly Haines*

Bottom left: One of the Temuka Methodist church members Ken Lee delivering Meals on Wheels to the Wallingford Aged Persons Home in his four-wheel drive Subaru. *Peter Butler*

Bottom right: Bruce Scott shovelling snow from his path, Lake Tekapo. *Elizabeth Scott*

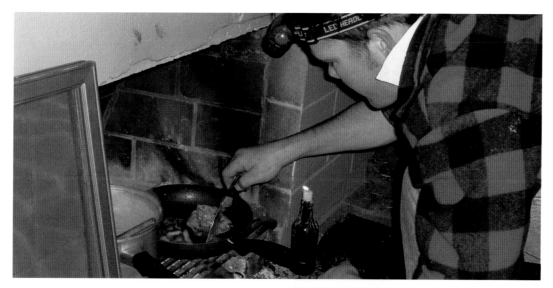

Top: Joe Redwood of Craigmore cooking on the open fire. Note the miner's lamp.
Joseph Redwood
Far left: Erin McBride cooking the evening meal in very cold conditions, Pinewood Motel, Winchester.
Kerry McBride
Left: John Hewson, 80 years old, of Seadown cooking his breakfast.
Bev Hewson

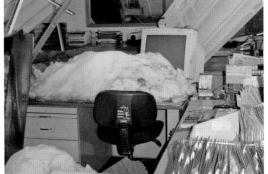

Extensive damage
to Hervey Motor's
showroom in Timaru,
probably the greatest
damage done to any
commercial building
during the storm.
Hervey Motors

Top: Spurwing plovers keeping one foot warm. *Alan Macnaughton*
Far left: Gizmo the kitten chasing goldfish through the ice on the fishpond, Temuka. *Sarah Archibald*
Left: Shetland ponies on the downs at Geraldine. Home was nothing like this. *Eamon Barrett*

Top: Scvcn Oaks cottage, Terrace Downs Resort, Lake Coleridge.
Nigel Armstrong
Right: Lake Clearwater frozen solid.
Sharon Attwood

Top: A huge igloo built by the five Smith children, Joshua, Daniel, Priscilla, Michael and Ruth, Temuka. Daniel is peeping over the top.
Elizabeth Smith
Far left: Snow hut built by the Tucker children, Timaru.
Tucker family
Left: Matthew Linton fishing outside his igloo, Fairview, Timaru.
Robert & Chrissy Linton

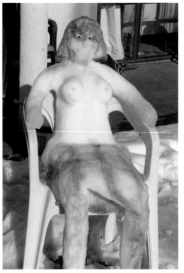

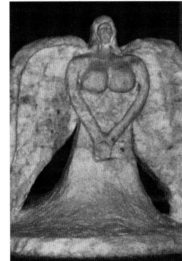

Top left: Pop and Carolyn Rosling's twin granddaughters beside the snowman their pop made for them, Ohoka, Kaiapoi.
Carolyn Rosling
Top right: Snow mannequin, imaginatively clothed.
Megan & Margaret Kane
Bottom left: Snow angel, Timaru.
Neal & Diane Hooper
Bottom right: Jacob White of Orari and his snowman.
Jill White

Far left: Guardian angel
at Pleasant
Point cemetery.
Jeff Tollan
Left: Robbie
Burns with a snow
mantle, Botanical
Gardens, Timaru.
Mark Low

Above: Surreal
gum trees.
Phil Keene
Right: Hoar frost,
Cowans Hill,
Mackenzie Country.
Sheila Preston

Stalactites of ice formed after minus 12- to 15-degree frosts.
Top: *Haidee & Al McCabe*
Left: *Jill White*

Top left: Ben James skiing on Caroline Bay !!!
Leigh James
Top right: Luke Lennox off the roof into West End Park, Timaru.
Gareth Hutton
Bottom left: Towing snowboarders in Salisbury Road, Timaru.
Lorraine Gibb
Bottom right: Jimmy Wright snowboarding in the Aoraki Polytech grounds.
Gareth Hutton
Right-hand page: Stormy skies over Lake Tekapo.
Kerry Mitchell

Top: Historic lighthouse,
Maori Park, Timaru.
Geoff Cloake
Right: Across the bay
to Timaru.
Geoff Cloake

Top left: Caroline Bay from the Benvenue walkway.
Lorraine McCarthy
Top right: The port of Timaru enjoys some brief sunlight.
Norm & Bev Clayton
Bottom left: Caroline Bay aviary – did the birds get snowed on?
Fraser family
Bottom right: The sails are down at Caroline Bay.
Fraser family

Left top and bottom:
Avalanche off the roof
at Melcombe Street,
Ashburton. Clearing
a path afterwards.
Christine Wilson
Top right: Trying to
take the dog for a walk.
Sheila Preston
Bottom right:
Halley Terrace, Temuka,
looking south.
C & V Howey
Right-hand page: The
eastern shore of Lake
Opuha, four weeks after
the big storm.
Greta Howey

Top left: The Miller family, Shawn, Alysha and Cameron, enjoy an outdoor picnic, Timaru.
Lynley Miller
Top right: The fridge! No power in Cricklewood.
Marielle Venrooy
Bottom left: Snowman, Lyall Terrace, Temuka.
C & V Howey
Bottom right: Snowman, Douglas Street, Timaru.
Michael Cullen
Left-hand page: Snow-covered Caroline Bay.
Norm & Bev Clayton

Top: Aerial view
of Tekapo.
Franka Morik
Bottom: Raewyn
Keene heading for the
Church of the Good
Shepherd, Tekapo.
Phil Keene

Two contrasting views of
Lake Tekapo.
Top: *Franka Morik*
Bottom: *Father Michael Pui*

Top: Amazing snow cover at Fox Peak snowfield.
Peter Wilkinson
Left: Joanna Gray inspecting the damage. Tobogganing down Priest Hill, Geraldine.
Philip Gray
Left-hand page: Castle Hill Station.
John Bougen

Top: Fashioning a passing lane on the road between Twizel and Tekapo. The road was open, but still down to one lane.
Phil Keene
Right: Road closed, looking east down Harris Street, Pleasant Point.
Jeff Tollan

Power lines down everywhere.
Top left: Otipua.
Megan Kane
Top right: Timaru.
Douglass family
Bottom left: Tekapo
Sheila Preston
Bottom right:
Albury substation.
Robert Tallett

Top: Ian & Jenny Smith's Deer, Peel Forest.
Alan Macnaughtan
Far Right: Knee-deep in snow, Brockley Road, Timaru.
Lindsay Coulter
Right: Ducks in frozen pond, Reflection Place, Coniston Water, Ashburton.
Kelly Haines
Right-hand page: Seadown, where the snow met the sea.
Bev Hewson

Top: Hannah Day
boogie-boarding in
the snow.
Hannah Day
Far right: Getting
towed. Clare and Amelia
Wilkinson at Fox Peak.
Peter Wilkinson
Right: Hayden Kerr in
the lawnmower catcher.
Kim Kerr
Right-hand page:
Snow ghosts.
Elizabeth Scott

Top and bottom left:
Sefton Street, early
morning and later in
the day.
Dave Jack
Top right: Albert
Street, Timaru.
Fraser family
Bottom right:
Nile Street, Timaru.
Lisa Marie Hejl

Top: A view
of Timaru looking north
from the hospital.
Nathan Taylor
Far left: Timaru,
looking over the
Botanical Gardens
to the Hunter Hills.
Nathan Taylor
Left: Timaru
from the air.
Matthew Dey

Top: Hanmer Springs.
Michael Simpson
Far right: Towards Waihaorunga from Mt Harris, looking over the Waihao Downs.
Edith Cromie
Right: The snow was deep at Cricklewood, Fairlie Basin.
Marielle Venrooy

Top: Waxeyes feeding – lucky for some. *Nigel Gamble*
Far left: The ducks are confused, ice-covered pond, Graham and Sharon Pecks property, Glen Hays, Totara Valley. *Nigel Gamble*
Left: Avenue of mature oak trees, Otumarama, Timaru. *Susie & Gerald Morton*

Top: An air-conditioned drive, Timaru.
Lindsay Coulter
Right: Going nowhere, Ashburton. Mt Somers in the background.
Selina Baker

Top: Damage to Mackenzie Services, Temuka. *Keith Woodhead*
Far left: Looking east down Wilmhurst Street, Temuka, towards the Presbyterian church. *Debbie & Brian Doake*
Left: At least the Speights is cold at the Arowhenua Hotel. *Jane Mullins*

Top: Lake Opua,
half-frozen.
Peter Wilkinson
Right: Cemetery Hill,
Pleasant Point.
Jeff Tollan

Top: Breaking up the snow, Keen Road, Orari Bridge, Timaru. *Lindsay Coulter*
Left: Railway wagons, Timaru. *Mark Low*

Top: A mob of 2000 Perendale sheep moving downhill to safety. The snow-raked trails form a pattern like a braided river, Matahiwi, Geraldine.
K Christie

Right: Hereford and Angus cows and calves being mustered down to lower country, looking towards Fairlie.
K Christie

Right-hand page: Danielle Daly-Lemon flat-land skiing at Lauriston, Mid-Canterbury.
Kerri Lemon

Left: Ten below at
Twizel, 26 June 2006.
Cheryl Doherty
Right: A foot of
snow, Orari.
Jill White